Classical Ballet Fundamentals

•

A Visual Guide

by

Charlotte R. Richards

Table of Contents

From the Author

This Visual Guide illustrates the classical body positions that are fundamental to Ballet expression onstage and in the studio. The book is organized into traditional categories showing positions of the feet, positions of the arms, head positions center and barre, the nine body directions and basic arabesque, all clearly shown in the artist's original hand-drawn slides.

Here you will find a quick reference essential for any serious young student training in the traditional classical form. College students, working dancers, and those who simply enjoy Ballet will recognize in these pages the foundation of traditional ballet movements, all of which spring from the classical positions pictured here. Small differences in terminology will vary among the individual systems.

For the attentive ballet student, use of this guide will add much to regular studies with any reputable ballet teacher.

— C.R.R.

Positions of the Feet

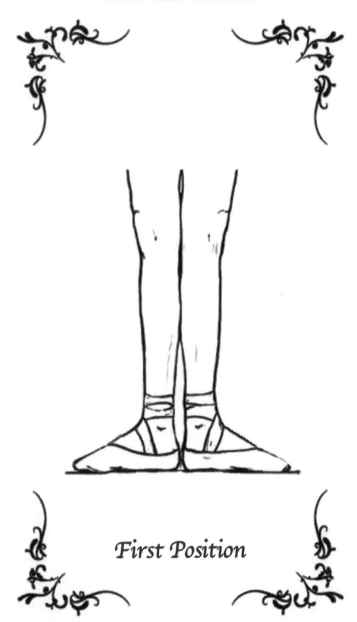

First Position

Second Position

Third Position

Fourth Position

Fifth Position

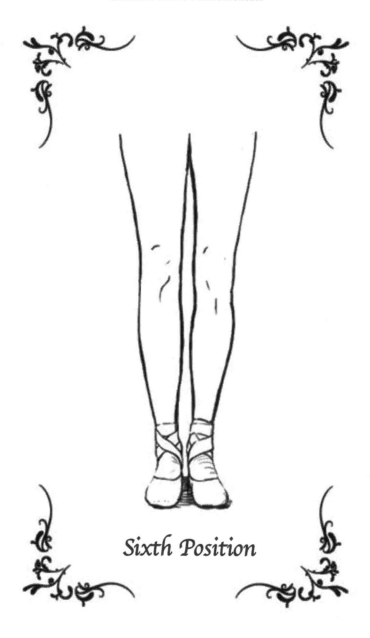

Sixth Position

Notes

Positions of the Arms

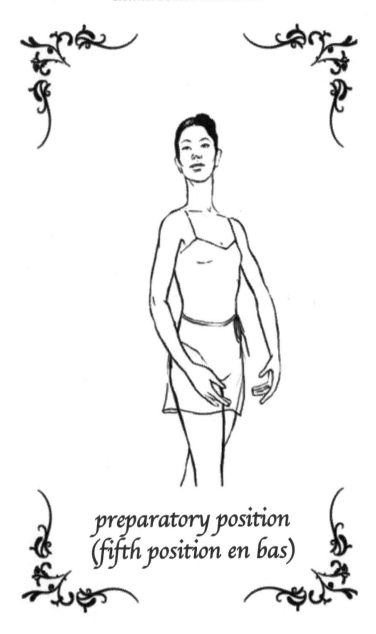

*preparatory position
(fifth position en bas)*

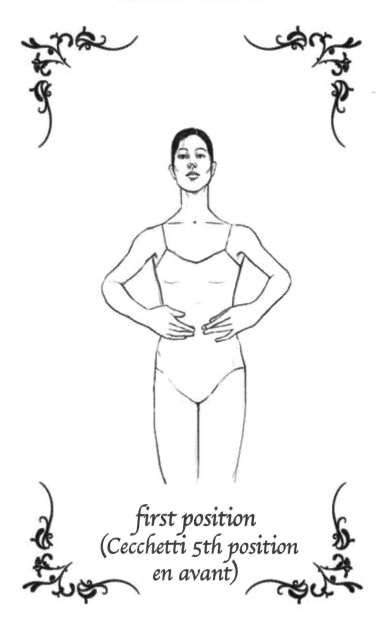

first position
(Cecchetti 5th position
en avant)

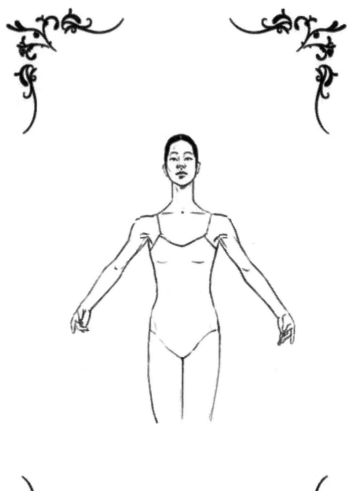

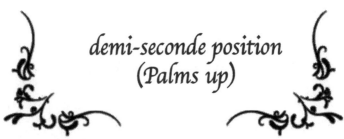

demi-seconde position
(Palms up)

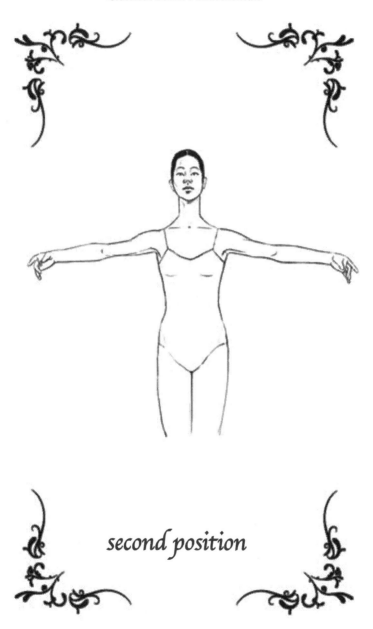

second position

third position low

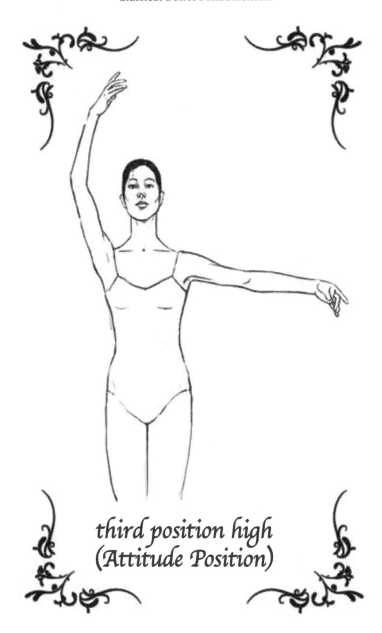

third position high
(Attitude Position)

fourth position

*fifh position
(en haut)*

Notes

Basic Arabesque

First Arabesque

Second Arabesque

Third Arabesque

Arabesque à Deux Bras
(Cecchetti 3rd Arabesque)

Fourth Arabesque

attitude croisé devant
(ah-tee-tewd krwah-say
duh-vahn)

attitude croisé derrière
(at-tee-tewd krwah-say
deh-ryehr)

B+
attitude à terre

Notes

Nine directions of the body
with translations

These 9 body positions comprise the basis of ballet tradition and technique. The torso and legs are placed oriented to the audience or the front of studio, and from these positions many changes are possible for the arms and head.

PAGE

See Reference Image p61:
   The Dancer's Personal Square

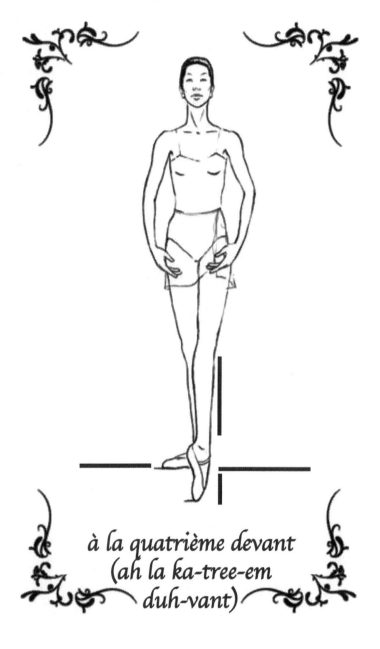

à la quatrième devant
(ah la ka-tree-em
duh-vant)

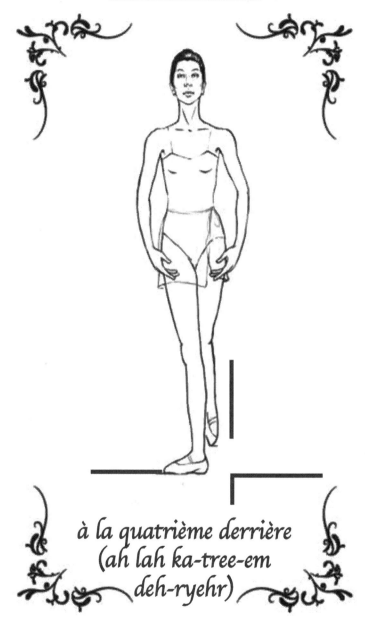

à la quatrième derrière
(ah lah ka-tree-em
deh-ryehr)

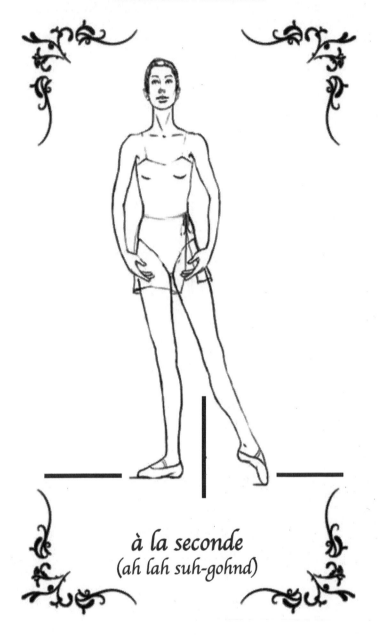

à la seconde
(ah lah suh-gohnd)

croisé devant
(krwah-say duh-vahn)

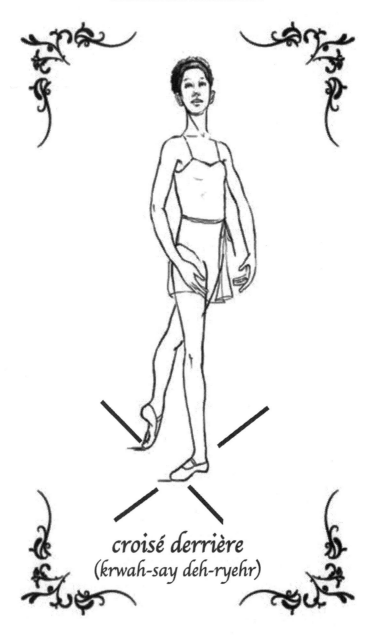

croisé derrière
(krwah-say deh-ryehr)

effacé devant
(ay-fah-say duh-vahn)

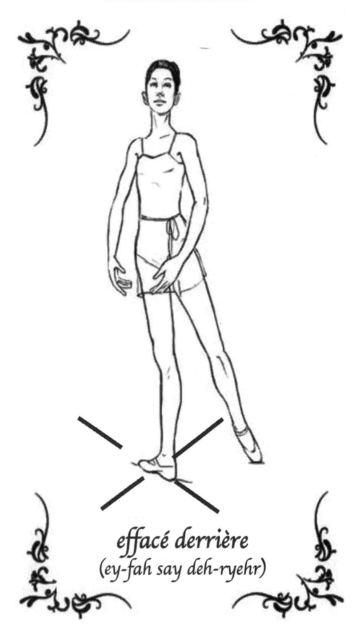

effacé derrière
(ey-fah say deh-ryehr)

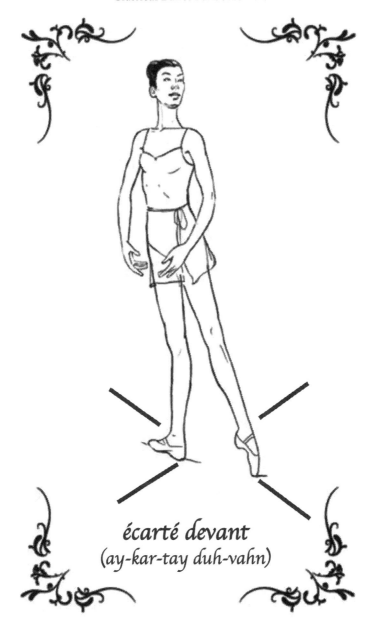

écarté devant
(ay-kar-tay duh-vahn)

écarté derrière
(ay-kar-tay deh-ryehr)

Basic Positions of the Head

Notes

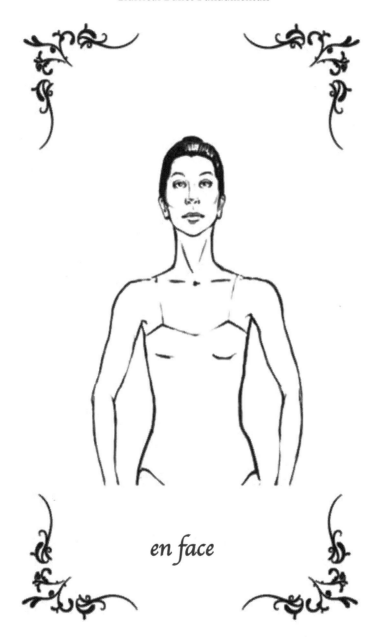

en face

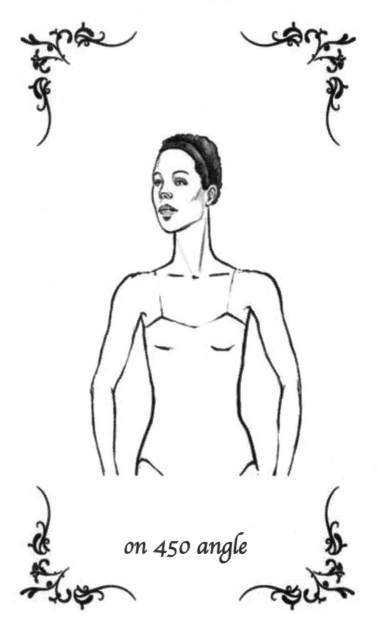

on 450 angle

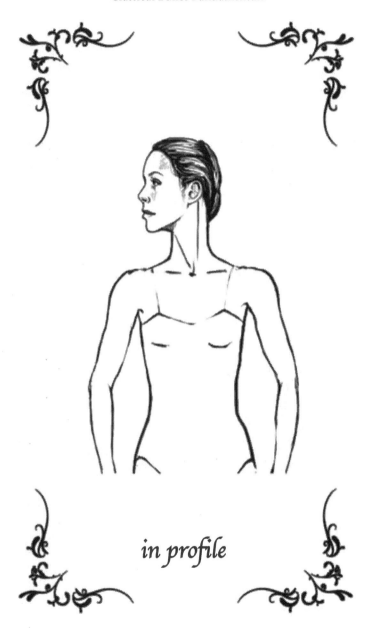

in profile

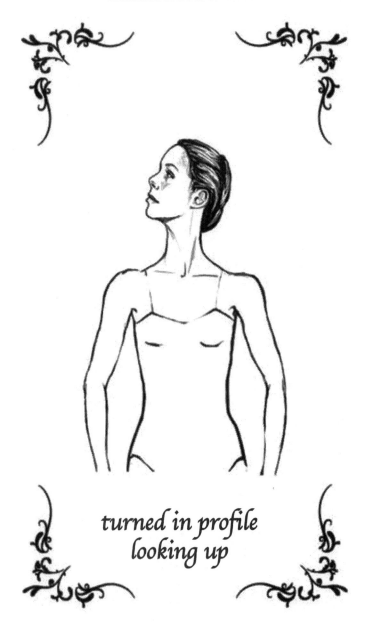

*turned in profile
looking up*

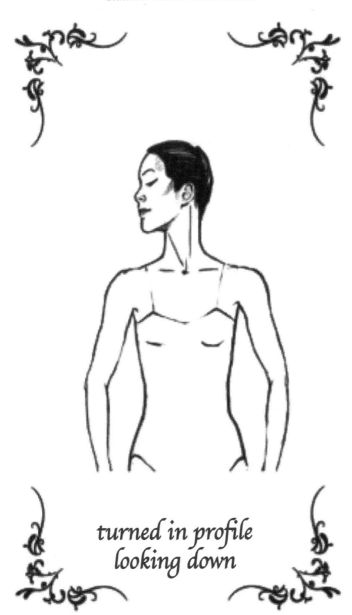

turned in profile
looking down

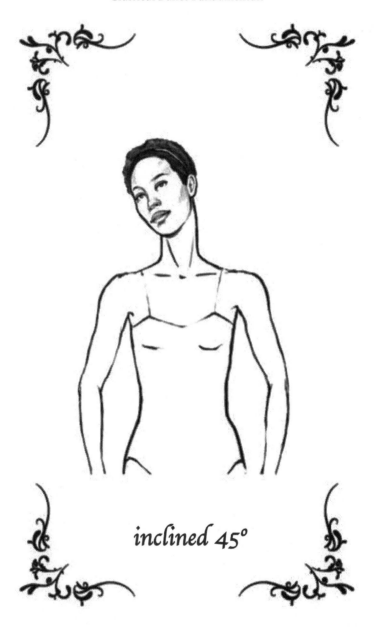

inclined 45°

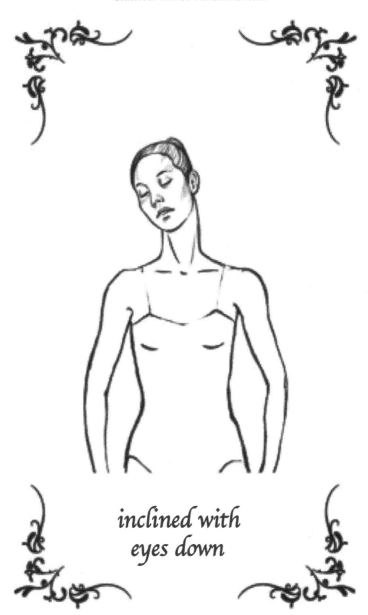

*inclined with
eyes down*

Notes

Heads at Barre

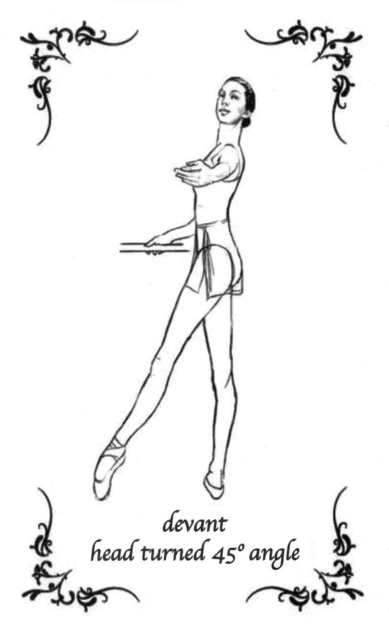

devant
head turned 45° angle

à la seconde
head erect facing front

derrière
head inclined forward
and turned

derrière

head turned at 45° toward
the barre
(without inclination)

Notes

Reference & Index

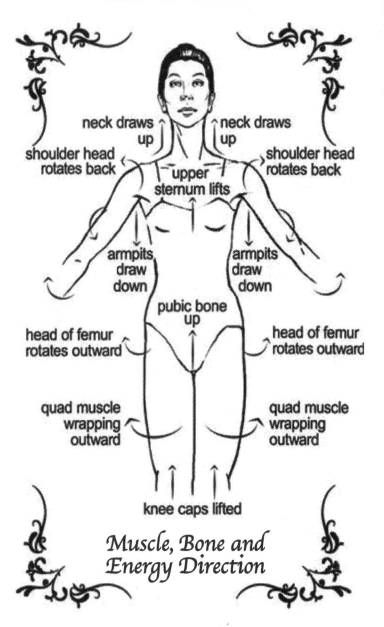

neck draws up

neck draws up

shoulder head rotates back

shoulder head rotates back

upper sternum lifts

armpits draw down

armpits draw down

pubic bone up

head of femur rotates outward

head of femur rotates outward

quad muscle wrapping outward

quad muscle wrapping outward

knee caps lifted

Muscle, Bone and Energy Direction

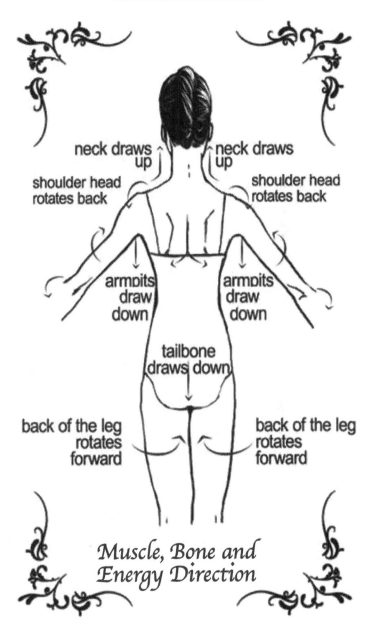

neck draws up

neck draws up

shoulder head rotates back

shoulder head rotates back

armpits draw down

armpits draw down

tailbone draws down

back of the leg rotates forward

back of the leg rotates forward

Muscle, Bone and Energy Direction

Turnout is an action.

The head of the femur bone rotates outward in the hip socket by means of the six deep rotator muscles under the gluteus. The thigh muscle lifts and wraps outward and the knee, ankle and foot together add further rotation, turning the whole leg as one. Thus, turnout starts from the hips, not from the feet.

Placement is the relationship of each part of the body to the next, in positions and in movement. This illustration shows the transfer of body weight maintaining placement.

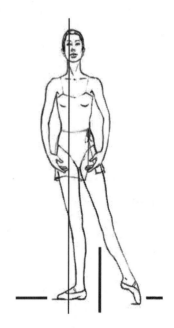

Vocabulary

Arabesque (ah-rah-BESK) – a spiral pose from Moorish architectural designs

Arrière, en (ah nah-RYEHR) – traveling backward

Attitude (ah-tee-TEWD) – positions suggested in classic images of Mercury the messenger god

Avant, en (ah na-VAHN) – traveling forward

Ballon (ba-LAWN) — rebound, lightness

Barre (bar) — horizontal bar held for support; exercises performed at the beginning of every class

Bas, en (ahn bah) – low

Battement (bat-MAHN) — beating; an action of leg(s)

Cambré (kahm-BRAY) —arched

Côté, de (duh koh-TAY) – traveling to the side

Croix, en (ahn KRAWH) – in the shape of a cross

Dedans, en (ahn duh-DAHN) – inward

Dehors, en (ahn duh-OR) – outward

Demi (duh-MEE) — half

Derrière (deh-RYEHR) – behind, in back

Diagonale, en (ahn dya-guh-NAL) – traveling in a diagonal line across the stage or studio

Dessous (duh-SOO) – under

Dessus (duh-SEW) – over

Devant (duh-VAHN) – in front

Face, en (ahn-FAHSS) – facing (the audience or front of studio)

Haut, en (ahn oh) – high

Passé (pah-SAY) – passed

Port de bras (pawr-duh-BRAH) – carriage of the arms

Port de corps (pawr-duh-KAWR) — carriage of the body

Retiré (ruh-tee-RAY) – withdrawn

Rèvèrence (reh-vah-RAHNSS) — to bow

Supporting leg – the leg which supports the body

Working leg – the leg that executes a given movement

Concepts & Objectives of Barre Work

- **plié**, bend — to warm up quads, hips, knees and ankles; to develop lightness in legs (ballon)
- **battement tendu**, stretch — to strengthen muscles of ankle and foot
- **battement dégagé**, disengage — to strengthen muscles in the foot and develop speed in the legs (in the Russian syllabus this is 'battement tendu jeté'; in the English school, 'battement glissé')
- **rond de jambe par terre**, round of leg on floor — to work on outward hip rotation (turnout)
- **rond de jambe en l'air**, round of leg in the air — to develop strength and precise movement in the knee joint
- **battement frappé**, strike or knock — to strengthen the intrinsic muscles of the foot for jumping
- **battement fondu**, melt — to gain strength and control of legs and feet, essential for entering and landing of jumps
- **petit battement**, little beat — for speed and precision of lower leg
- **grand battement**, large beat — to strengthen hip muscles and limber the joints for développé and large jumps

Fixed Points of Stage & Studio

— Cecchetti system —

Downstage Left   Downstage Right

2	5	1
6		8
3	7	4

Upstage Left   Upstage Right

Fixed Points of Stage & Studio

— Russian system —

Downstage Left   Downstage Right

8	1	2
7		3
6	5	4

Upstage Left   Upstage Right

The Dancer's Personal Square
— Body Directions—

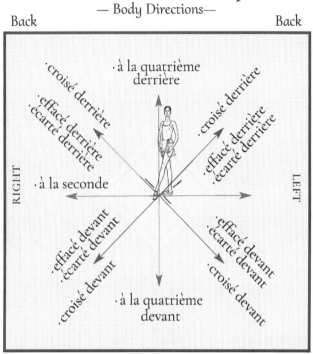

Back   Back

à la quatrième derrière

·croisé derrière

·effacé derrière
·écarté derrière

·croisé derrière

·effacé derrière
·écarté derrière

RIGHT

·à la seconde

LEFT

·effacé devant
·écarté devant

·croisé devant

·effacé devant
·écarté devant

·croisé devant

à la quatrième devant

Front   Front

Dancer is depicted *croisé devant* (on a diagonal line), left leg Front. Alternately, body direction *effacé devant* would be facing the same diagonal, with right leg Front. *Derrière* of these positions, opposite leg is Back. Still facing the diagonal, placing leg (L. or R.) to Side, you have *écarté*. Torso facing front, leg placed front or back is *à la quatrième devant* or *derrière*. Leg placed Side L. or R. is *à la seconde*.

Index

Attitude
25 attitude croisé devant
26 attitude croisé derrière
27 B+ attitude à terre

Nine directions of the body,
    —*with translations*—
31 À la quatrième devant
    to the fourth, front
32 À la quatrième derrière
    to the fourth, back
33 À la seconde
    to the second
34 Croisé devant
    crossed front
35 Croisé derrière
    crossed back
36 Effacé devant
    shaded front
37 Effacé derrière
    shaded back
38 Écarté devant
    thrown apart front (downstage)
39 Écarté derrière
    thrown apart back (upstage)

Classical Ballet Fundamentals

Acknowledgments

BOOK ILLUSTRATIONS
INA LIM with Erin McClain

PLATINUM SWAN LOGO DESIGN
Mark Byrne

ART PRODUCTION DIRECTOR
Dante Sefas

EBOOK LAYOUT FOR THE 3RD EDITION
Dan Davies

Special thanks to Bill and Justice
for all their good work and support

et bien sûr, Tricia

interior text
Cormorant Garamond

71

Notes

Made in the USA
Columbia, SC
21 March 2023

14086196R00048